This book is dedicated to Aline

"Pour Eternité"

The author of this book Benjamin James Baillie lives and works in Normandy

Richard the Lionheart

THE LAST WAR
1194 - 1199 AD

By Benjamin James Baillie

Contents

INTRODUCTION 911-1192 A.D

The seeds of Discontent
The Angevin Empire
The Devils Brood
The King is dead, long live the King
The Third Crusade
The Devil is loosed

NORMANDY 1194-1199 A.D

1194 AD
Return of the King: Barfleur
Siege of Verneuil Sur Avre
Battle of Freteval
1195 AD
Total War
Vaudreuil
1196 AD
My beautiful Daughter
Château Gaillard (le Roche d'Andeli)
1197 AD
The wheel of fortune turns against Philip
Beauvais and Milly
Flanders
1198 AD
The Lion and the Lamb
The battle of Gisors
Like a hungry Lion upon its prey
1199 AD
Peace and the end of the Lionheart
Legend of the lost gold
Aftermath

INTRODUCTION

Follow in the footsteps of Richard "the Lionheart" one of the most renowned warrior heroes of all time. His exploits during the Third Crusade gained him eternal fame and a fearsome reputation both in Europe and beyond, but it was his last military campaign in Normandy that required all his experience and skill as a general and King to overturn the territory lost to the French King Philip Augustus during his imprisonment by the German Emperor on returning home from the Holy land. Normandy was the linchpin in the vast Angevin Empire which stretched from the foothills of the Pyrenees to the border with Scotland. It was also the ancestral heartland of the Anglo-Norman aristocracy who still regarded the fertile Duchy as "home". From 1194 – 1199 AD it was the battleground between Christendom's two bitterest enemies. In the age of Robin Hood this book will bring to life Richard's "Last War" to recover and hold together the Angevin Empire in France which evokes all the emotion and courageous chivalry which earned him the nickname "Coeur de Lion / Lionheart".

Effigy of Richard I "Coeur de Lion" Fontevraud Abbey, Anjou

The seeds of Discontent
911 – 1192 AD

In order to understand the relationship between the Kings of England and France we must travel back in time to the creation of the Duchy of Normandy. During the 9th and 10th centuries Viking raiders from modern day Scandinavia terrorised most of mainland Europe and the British Isles. The French province of Neustria (North western France) suffered increased invasions and by 911 AD the King of Western France, Charles III "the Simple" had no choice but to cede the area of the Seine valley and coastal regions to the Viking Chief Rollo (Hrolfr).

The treaty of St Clair sur Epte has been shrouded in mystery ever since. Legend has it that during the conclusion of the treaty Charles demanded Rollo kiss his foot as an act of fealty and homage. Rollo refused but asked one of his subordinates to perform the duty in his place. The selected Viking warrior grabbed the King's foot and hurled him backwards in the air. Clearly vassal or no vassal Rollo and his war band were too powerful to be dictated to or punished.

The Duchy of Normandy had now been founded in which Rollo was baptised into Christianity, taking the name Robert. He married Poppa de Bayeux and in theory controlled the land as a subject vassal of the French King.

Over the next 150 years the Dukes of Normandy expanded their territory annexing lower Normandy, pushing the western borders with Brittany and encroaching on the disputed territory of Maine with the Counts of Anjou in the south. In 1034 AD the Vexin region between the river Epte and Oise was ceded over to Duke Robert "the Magnificent". This important region meant that the Normans were less than 60km away from the French capital of Paris. The French King Henry I tried to curtail Norman power by invading the Duchy in 1054 AD. His forces were defeated at the Battle of Mortemer and again at the decisive Battle of Varaville in 1057 AD.

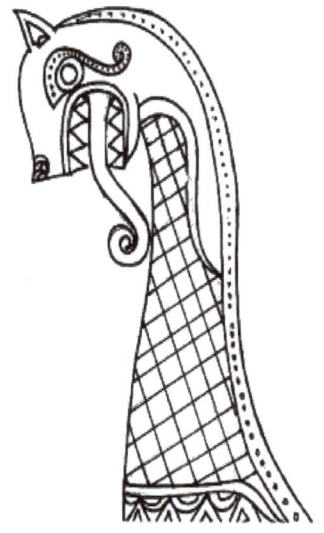

Free from anymore French aggression Duke William II invaded England and destroyed the army of the Anglo-Saxon King Harold II Godwinsson at the Battle of Hastings in 1066 AD. The Duke was crowned King William I at Westminster on Christmas day in 1066 AD and thus became the King of England as well as the Duke of Normandy.

The Norman conquest of England. The battle of Hastings 1066 (Bayeux Tapestry)

After William's death in 1087 A.D the crown and Dukedom passed to each of his sons, William II "Rufus", Robert "Curthose" and finally Henry I "Beauclerc". When Henry Beauclerc's son died in a shipwreck off the Norman coast, Henry forced the Anglo-Norman nobility to accept his daughter Matilda as heir. Upon the King's death, his nephew Stephen de Blois had other ideas and usurped the crown with the help of his brother, Henry of Winchester. For nineteen long years England was ravaged by civil war. Matilda with the help of her second husband Geoffrey Plantagenet (the Count of Anjou) fought on, but it was their son, Henry Plantagenet who forced Stephen accept his succession, finally ending the anarchy in 1154 A.D

The Angevin Empire
1152-1189 AD

Tombs of Henry Plantagenêt and Eleanor D' Aquitaine. (Fontevraud abbey, Anjou, France)

On the 18th of May 1152 AD Henry Plantagenet married Eleanor, the heiress to the Duchy of Aquitaine. On King Stephen's death in 1154 AD Henry became King of England, Duke of Normandy, through his mother, Count of Anjou, Touraine and Maine through his father, Duke of Aquitaine though Eleanor his wife and Overload of Brittany, Scotland, Wales and Ireland.

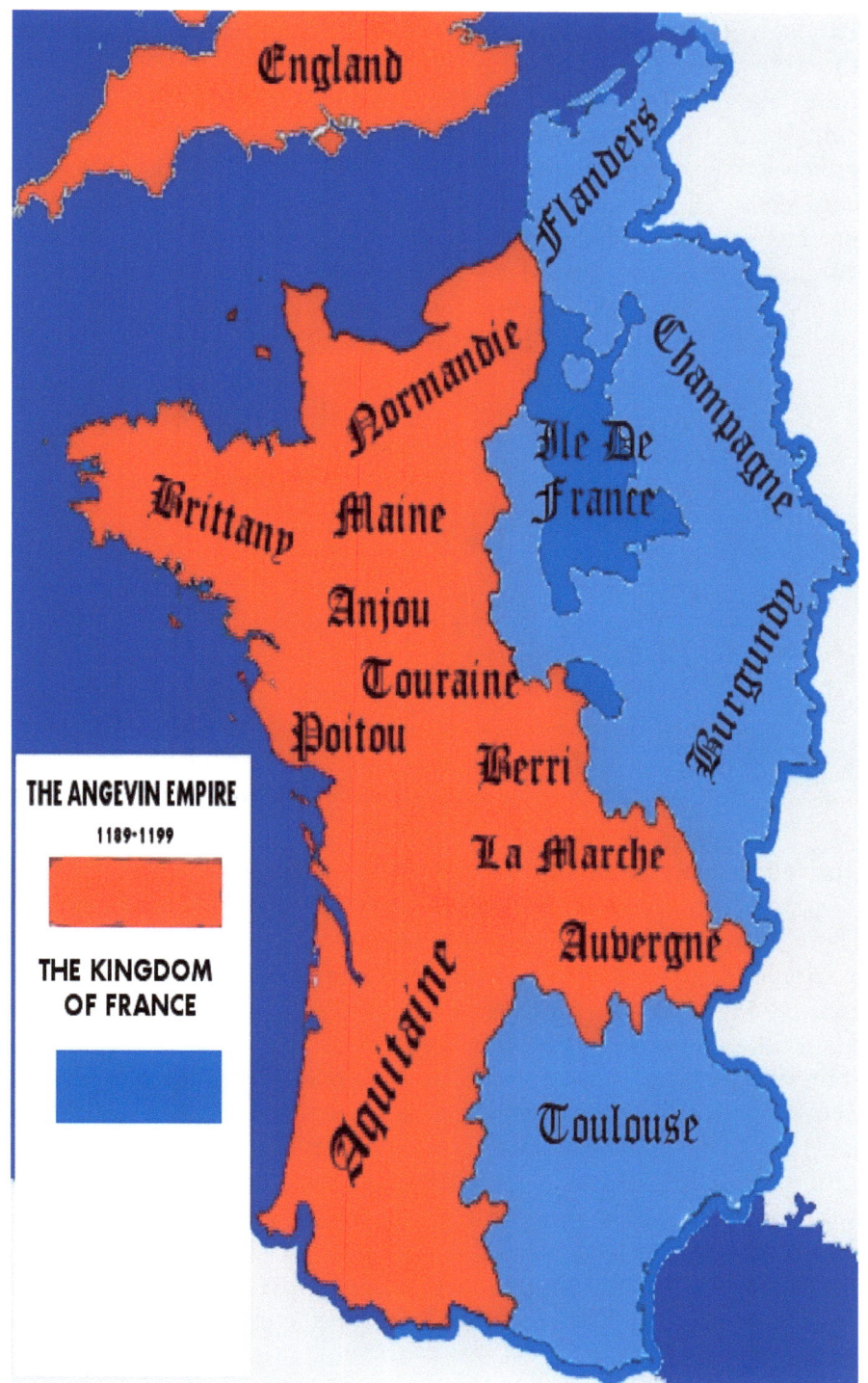

Although Henry was King of England, in France he was only a Duke /Count and therefore had to paid homage to the French King for those lands on the continent. The problem was Henry as a vassal had become more powerful than his liege lord. The Angevin Empire stretched for the borders of Scotland to the foothills of the Pyrenees and made Henry the most powerful monarch in Europe. The marriage between Henry and Eleanor produced no less than eight children who became known by the nickname "the devils brood".

The Devils Brood

Church carving of Melusine and the Plantagenet lion, Civray

There is an old legend that the houses of Anjou "the Angevins" were descended from the Devil himself. Supposedly an early Count married Melusine the daughter of Satan. This was only discovered when time and time again Melusine refused to attend mass in church until one day her husband forced her to stay during the service. Before the service was over, Melusine freed herself from her guards and flew through the window taking her two children with her never to be seen again. Although very dramatic in a time when superstition was much engrained in people's minds, this story stuck and was passed down from generation to generation. A possible truth may be that Melusine was from another faith and refused to attend mass for that reason, but we may never totally know the exact truth behind the legend.

From this legend the Angevins became known as the "Devils brood". There was also a curse that iterated that the Plantagenet's would destroy each other; father was to fight son and brother against brother. Richard the Lionheart encouraged the legend be even stating;

"From the Devil we sprang, and to the Devil we shall go".

The curse would indeed come true during the lifetime of King Henry II Plantagenet. After Prince John was born in 1167 AD Henry and Eleanor slowly grew apart. Eleanor spent most of her time in Aquitaine while Henry ruled his dominions travelling from region to region entertaining his famous mistress Rosemond Clifford (Fair Rosemond).

Eleanor d'Aquitaine

In 1172 AD Richard was made Duke of Aquitaine in Poitiers. The young King Henry (Henry's eldest son) would inherit England and Normandy, Brittany was to go to Geoffrey and the newly conquered Ireland to John. The only problem with this arrangement was that Henry II was still a young man only in his thirties and although he would give all his sons titles, he would not relinquish any of the real power.

During the last 20 years of Henry's reign he was plagued by rebellions fermented by his sons, his wife and the French monarchy eager to destroy the Angevin Empire once and for all.

Henry was a remarkable King and each time he crushed the plots and revolts against him using the vast resources of his Empire. Queen Eleanor was confined in England to deter her from causing any more trouble on the continent. In 1183 AD tragedy befell the King when his eldest son Henry (the young King) died. Three years later Geoffrey Duke of Brittany was killed in a tournament accident which only left Richard and John as his male heirs.

In 1188 A.D Henry was in Normandy fighting against the advances of the French King Philip Augustus. Rumours had been circulating from Paris that Henry intended to disinherit Richard in favour of John, his favourite and youngest son.

During the peace negotiations in November the French King Philip Augustus proposed that the postponed marriage between his sister Alice (Countess of the Vexin) and Richard should take place immediately, the disputed areas should be given to Richard and that Henry should publicly acknowledge Richard as his successor. Clearly the French King was eager to force a rift between father and son.

Henry played into the hands of the French King and confirmed Richard's fears by refusing to acknowledge the conditions. Richard felt betrayed and paid homage to King Philip for all his continental possessions. Philip had succeeded in forcing a rift between father and son, and by 1189 A.D they had openly declared war on the aged Plantagenet King. Henry's once famed un-bounding energy was ebbing away, meanwhile Richard had become an experienced military commander during the years of civil war. The conqueror of the impregnable castle of Taillebourg had now come of age.

In the summer of 1189 A.D Richard and Philip invaded Maine. The local nobility loyal to Henry changed sides believing that the old King would soon be dead.

Geoffrey Plantagenet (father of Henry II)

Palais of the Counts du Maine (Le Mans) France
Henry Plantagenet's birthplace

While at Le Mans (Henry's birthplace) the Franco-rebel alliance caught up with the King. Henry rather than face a siege, ill like a wounded lion withdrew and ordered Le Mans to be burned to the ground to slow down his enemies. First heading north for the safety of Normandy, he was forced to turn south back into Anjou when news reached him that the major routes into Normandy had been captured by the rebels.

Richard chased after his father on route to Chinon (Henry's ancestral stronghold in Anjou) to force him into submission, but the King's entourage was led by Sir William Marshal (the champion of over 500 tournaments and one of the most feared knights in Christendom). Marshal was Henry's most loyal knight and decided to protect the King at all costs by riding back towards the enemy to orchestrate an ambush. As Richard and his knights closed in on the Royal entourage, he was surprised by Marshal and the loyalist bodyguard.

Sir William Marshal charged into the melee unhorsed Richard in the process. Only a last minute cry from Richard:

"By God's legs Marshal, do not kill me, I am unarmed"

saved his life as the Marshal re-aimed his lace, killing Richard's horse and not the Duke himself.

Marshal replied:
"I will not kill you, but the Devil may"

Although Marshal's actions saved the King from certain capture, Henry's enemies were closing in on Chinon. Unable to escape north towards Normandy and England he was forced to capitulate.
On the 4th of July at Azay le Rideau Henry was forced to accept the humiliating conditions imposed on him by his son and the French King. A broken man he returned back to Chinon in a litter, desperately ill. When reading the list of pardons of those who had conspired against him, he saw John's name. His favourite son had turned traitor against him. Just before he died he turned to Geoffrey his illegitimate son and said **"The others are the real bastards"**. So the life of the grandfather of Europe came to an end.

Sir William Marshal

The King is dead, long live the King

Henry's body was taken the short distance from the castle of Chinon to the Abbey of Fontevraud in the heart of Anjou to be buried. Richard followed the procession, entered the Abbey and paid his respects to his father, whom he had betrayed.

After the funeral Richard rode north to Normandy, to assert his authority. In the cathedral of Rouen he was invested with the Ducal sword, and crowned Duke of Normandy. While crossing the river Seine near Pont de l'Arche he got caught in the current and nearly drowned. On reaching the safety of the river bank, he gave thanks for this good fortune by founding the Abbey of Bonport. The coronation in England followed and by 1190 AD Richard was again back in France preparing the final details for the Third Crusade to recover the Holy land from the Saracens. The French King Philip Augustus had also agreed to take the cross and joined Richard in Vezelay to disuse the strategy and details of the campaign.

The castle of Chinon (Anjou) France

Had the events at the Battle of Hattin (1187 AD) and the fall of Jerusalem not happened, it is fairly likely to say that war between Richard and Philip would have started as early as 1190-91. AD.

King Philip's lifelong ambition was to destroy the power of the Angevin Empire, King Henry was gone, but Richard had now stepped into his father's shoes, thus making him Philips rival and enemy. However for the time being the two rulers concentrated their energy on the fore coming Crusade.

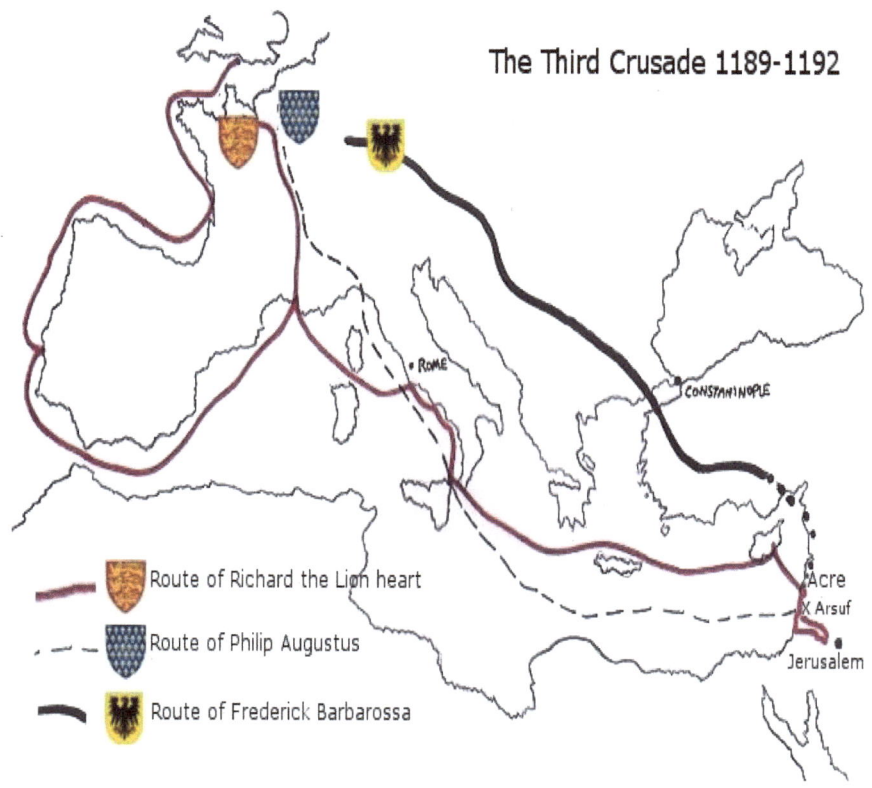

The Third Crusade
1189-1192 AD

As well as the Kings of England and France, the Crusade was joined by Frederick Barbarossa "the Holy Roman Emperor". The Three most powerful monarchs in Europe embarked on the Third Crusade. Barbarossa chose the land route across the Byzantine Empire, but in a freak accident he drowned while crossing the river Saleph in Turkey. The remnants of his army reached the Holy land under the banner of his son Henry of Swabia, who then passed overall command of the German contingent to Leopold Duke of Austria.

Richard and Philip left Vezelay on July 1st 1190 AD and chose sea routes towards the Holy land.

The Angevin and French fleets arrived at the half way point in Sicily during a crucial time in the island's history. The Normans under the De Hauteville family had conquered most of Southern Italy and Sicily only a century before **(further reading in my book "The First Mafia" The Norman Conquest of Southern Italy and Sicily)** and Richard's sister Joan had been married to King William II "the Good", but after his death the new King, Tancred de Lecce imprisoned Joan and withheld her dowry. Richard threatened Tancred with invasion unless he released Joan and submit. As a show of intent he captured and sacked the important port of Messina. Tancred realising he might loss his crown and also his head quickly backed down and gave into Richard's demands.

While on the island Philip again raised the question of the marriage between Richard and Alice, but Richard refused to commit on the grounds that Alice had been an alleged mistress of his father Henry and that they had an illegitimate child together. In fact Eleanor of Aquitaine had been secretly negotiating with the King of Navarre to marry his daughter Berengaria to Richard (this marriage would secure the Duchy of Aquitaine from French advances).

Hauteville Arms, Montreal Sicily

Finally in March 1191 AD the two fleets set sail from Sicily for the Holy land. During a storm Richard's fleet was scattered and after some shipwrecked survivors from the fleet were roughly treated by a rebel Byzantine regime in Cyprus Richard decided to conquer the island. In strategic terms, the conquest of Cyprus secured an offshore base for the Crusaders and the imperiled Christian states of the Outremer.

While in Cyprus Richard's bride arrived and the happy couple were married in St George's chapel Limassol by the Bishop of Evreux. After the marriage, Cyprus was handed over to Guy de Lusignan, one time King of Jerusalem and staunch ally of King Richard.

With the arrival of the fresh Crusader armies, the coastal city of Acre which was already under siege finally surrendered. As the Crusaders took control of the city they placed the banners of King Richard, King Philip Augustus and Duke Leopold on the battements, but Richard hauled down of Duke Leopold's banner acclaiming it had no place to be with that of a King, this insensitive incident would have repercussions later.

Both Richard and Philip contracted dysentery during the siege. In the pact at Vezelay, the two Kings agreed the split the profits of the campaign 50/50, but ill feeling over the spoils of war erupted into open disagreement. Firstly Philip demanded half of Cyprus, then Richard counter claimed that he should be given half of Artois in France whose Lord had just died during the siege of Acre. Feeling overshadowed by the Lionheart, King Philip tired of the whole campaign and decided to return home to France.

King Richard (left) and King Philip accepting the keys to Acre

Before he left, he promised Richard he would not attack any of his lands in France. With the French King out of the way Richard took control of the remaining Crusaders and marched on to capture the coastal cities of Caesarea, Jaffa, Ramleh, Ibelin, Darum and Ascalon. He defeated Saladin at the Battle of Arsuf, but was unable to take the ultimate prize of the holy city of Jerusalem. After many tiresome negotiations a three year truce was finally agreed. The details of which were that the Crusaders could kept the towns they had captured and more importantly that pilgrims were allowed to visit Jerusalem once again without fear of persecution. With the agreement ratified the Third Crusade was now at an end and Richard decided to return home to France. He had received disturbing reports that King Philip had already broken his word and was stirring up trouble on the borders of the Angevin Emprie.

On nearing the port of Marseilles Richard received word that the Count of Toulouse intended to arrest him and hand him over to King Philip Augustus for trial over an attack by Richard's Seneschal in Gascony on the Count's lands. Richard decided to sail on but headwinds stopped his

Arms of King Richard I based on an early seal

ships from attempting to circum navigate the Iberian Peninsula, thus the fleet turned about and headed for the Adriatic coast to return home via Germany. Richard traveled through Northern Italy and then Austria making for the lands of Henry "the Lion" (Duke of Saxony and Bavaria), his brother in law.

Austria was hostile territory and Richard's behavior towards its Duke (Leopold) during the Third Crusade only highlighted the danger in passing through the Duke's lands.

Richard travelled incognito with a few close companions disguised as pilgrims, but his lavish spending alerted the agents of the Duke. There were several close escapes, on one occasion a local Austrian lord sent out one of his retinue to inspect the party of pilgrims. The knight was originally from Normandy and when he discovered it was King Richard and his Duke, he broke down in tears of joy and supplied him with provisions and fresh horses in order to escape.

Seal of Henry the Lion (Duke of Saxony and Bavaria).

The capture of the Lionheart, prisoner in Germany

Richard's luck finally run out and he was arrested by Duke Leopold's men just outside Vienna and only 80km from the lands of his brother in law, Henry "the Lion". Leopold handed his valuable prisoner over to his liege lord Henry VI, "the Holy Roman Emperor". During this time King Philip could no longer resist the temptation of trying to dismantle the Angevin empire and unit France under his rule.

Richard's troublesome younger brother, Prince John needed little persuasion into establishing an alliance with King Philip. He immediately travelled to France and paid homage to him for all the Angevin lands on the continent and even the Kingdom of England. In 1193 AD while Richard was languishing in captivity Philip invaded the Duchy of Normandy. The important border castle of Gisors opened its gates to the French King without any resistance. Its Governor Gilbert Vascoeuil's name became a byword for treachery in the Duchy.

With the Vexin secured, Philip moved on to take the Norman capital Rouen, but the capital was defended by the experienced Crusader Robert Fitz Parnel (the Earl of Leicester) who when showed false documents from King Philip instructing him to hand over Rouen promptly replied;

The Medieval streets of Rouen, Normandy, France

"If you wish to enter, the gates are open"

King Philip smelling a trap decided against a direct assault or siege and withdrew back towards the border to consolidate his recent gains in the Vexin.

Richard's ransom was set at 100,000 marks, but King Philip and Prince John offered 150,000 marks to get their hands on the Lionheart. In the end only Richard's skill as a diplomat in resolving a dispute between the Emperor and rebel Princes from the Lower Rhineland compelled Henry VI to release him on the 14th March 1194 AD.

The Devil is Loosed

On hearing the news of Richard's release, King Philip wrote to John; **"Look to yourself, the Devil is loosed"**.

Richard returned to England after an absence of over four years and was re-crowned at Winchester in an elaborate ceremony. Almost immediately he set about securing England's northern border by pacifying the King of Scots, then reselling many lucrative offices and titles in order to raise the money he needed to regain the lost territories in France.

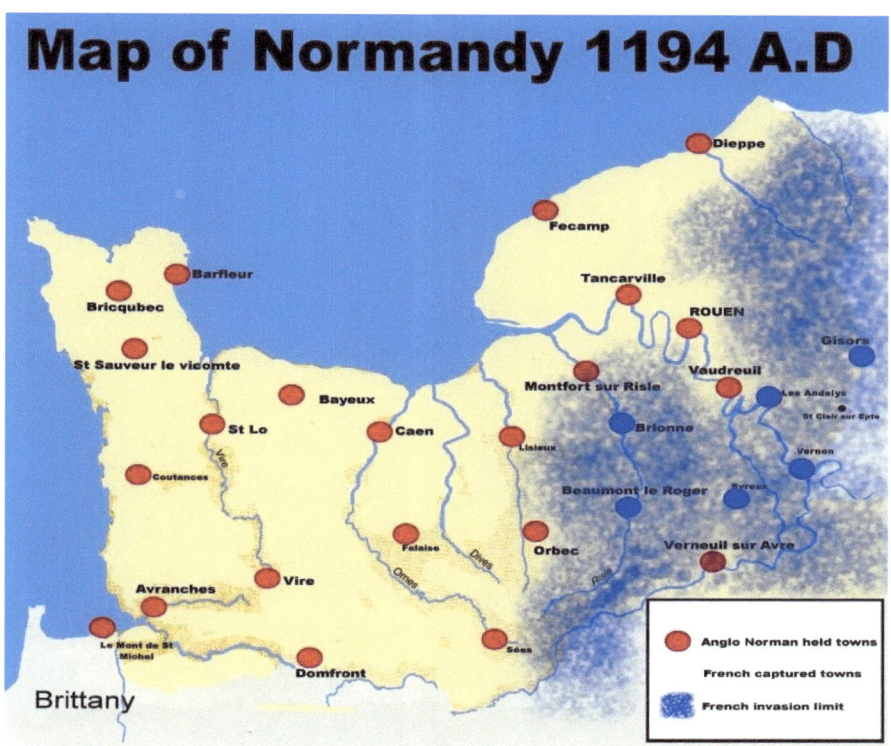

King Philip's invasion of 1193 AD had overrun the Vexin and most of Eastern Normandy. Richard's agents had secured a rest bite from further French advances at the Treaty of Mantes in July 1193 AD. The one sided treaty stipulated that Philip could keep all his recent territorial gains; Richard would also have to pay 20,000 marks and cede the great fortresses of Loches and Chatillon in Tourraine.

1194 AD, the year of reckoning had come. The last war in Normandy would require all of Richard's experience in both warfare and politics to regain the lost lands in the age before the invention of cannon, where the advantage favoured the defenders of strong castles and fortified towns.

King Richard I statue, London, England

Return of the King, Barfleur 1194 AD

In spring 1194 AD Richard left England for the last time and crossed the Channel to Normandy. The King arrived in Barfleur (Contentin, Lower Normandy) to a joyful welcome, old and young came out of their thatched houses to see their rightful Duke and the hero of the Third Crusade. The King was accompanied by his father's loyal lieutenant Sir William Marshal and many of the Anglo-Norman aristocracy eager to defend their Norman ancestral seats.

A retainer of Sir William Marshal who was present at Barfleur stated: **"God has come again in all his strength"**. The procession continued through the Contentin into Calvados where en route Prince John was reconciled with his brother Richard, begging for forgiveness. Richard pardoned his brother;
"Do not be afraid John, you are a child and have got into bad company"

The relief of Verneuil Sur Avre

Effigy of Richard at Verneuil sue Avre

Since February King Philip had been besieging the remaining Anglo-Norman strongholds on the Duchy's eastern frontier along the river Avre. By May only the border castle of Verneuil sur Avre stood in the way of King Philip controlling a line of fortresses following the river Iton, within striking distance to attack lower Normandy and the Ducal capital of Rouen. The castle garrison was so confident of withstanding the French assault that they even painted an unflattering image of Philip on their gates in defiance. When Richard heard the news he marched at once to relieve the siege.

He sent John to Evreux, where after pretending to be loyal to King Philip, John entered the town and had the French garrison executed. A gruesome tale circulated that the heads of the French soldiers were hung above the town gates. In an act of revenge King Philip left the siege of Verneuil in order to retake Evreux which he sacked, but the French army at Verneuil now leaderless broke off the siege when they heard the news that the Anglo-Norman army was approaching with the Lionheart at its head. Richard entered Verneuil at the end of May and personally thanked the castle defenders for their bravery in defending the town. With his supply lines cut King Philip had no choice but to retreat back over the border towards Paris.

Richard repaired and reinforced the town and castle walls before turning his attention south. In Tourraine he re-took the castles of Loches and Montmirail. Tours opened its gates without any struggle to its Angevin lord. Richard was intent on bringing order to the southern part of the Angevin Empire and punishing the rebel barons who were in open revolt and in league with the French King.

Loches castle, Anjou. Photograph by Michal Osmenda

While Richard was campaigning in the south, Philip instead of attending a peace conference arranged between the two parties in Pont de l'Arche near Rouen launched a destructive raid down the valley of the river Risle near Brionne. In June the French forces managed to capture the gallant defender of Rouen Robert Fitz Parnal (Beaumont), the Earl of Leicester, who was trying to retake the border castle of Pacy-sur-Eure. Robert remained in French captivity for the next three years.

The Battle of Fretéval, July 1194 AD

By July 1194 AD Richard had all but extinguished the last sparks of revolt in Angouleme and Aquitaine. Only the castles of Marcilliac and Tailleborg (the same castle Richard had captured when he was a young man) held out, but they were quickly reduced. The fortress of Angouleme was taken in a single evening, its fall signaled the pacification of the territories of the Count of Angouleme. Richard wrote back to England;

> "We have captured all the lands from our enemies and taken 300 knights captive".

Arms of Robert Fitz-Parnell (Beaumont) Earl of Leicester

As Richard returned north to ease the pressure on Normandy, Philip headed south likewise to ease the pressure on the rebel barons. The two armies were now on a direct collision course. Richard encamped at Vendome while Philip was only a few kilometers away at Fretéval. Philip was no warrior and although he sent word that he intended to give battle, in reality he struck camp not daring to risk a direct confrontation and retreated north. When Richard's spies reported that the French were retreating, Richard at once gave chase and on the 4th of July caught up with the rearguard of the French army.

So intense was his desire to capture or kill Philip that it is said when one horse tired he took another, searching for his mortal enemy. Philip only evaded capture by seeking refuge in a church as the battle was joined. Although the French King escaped, his baggage train, treasure and royal records did not (of which included important lists of those Angevin subjects who had betrayed or intended to join the French).

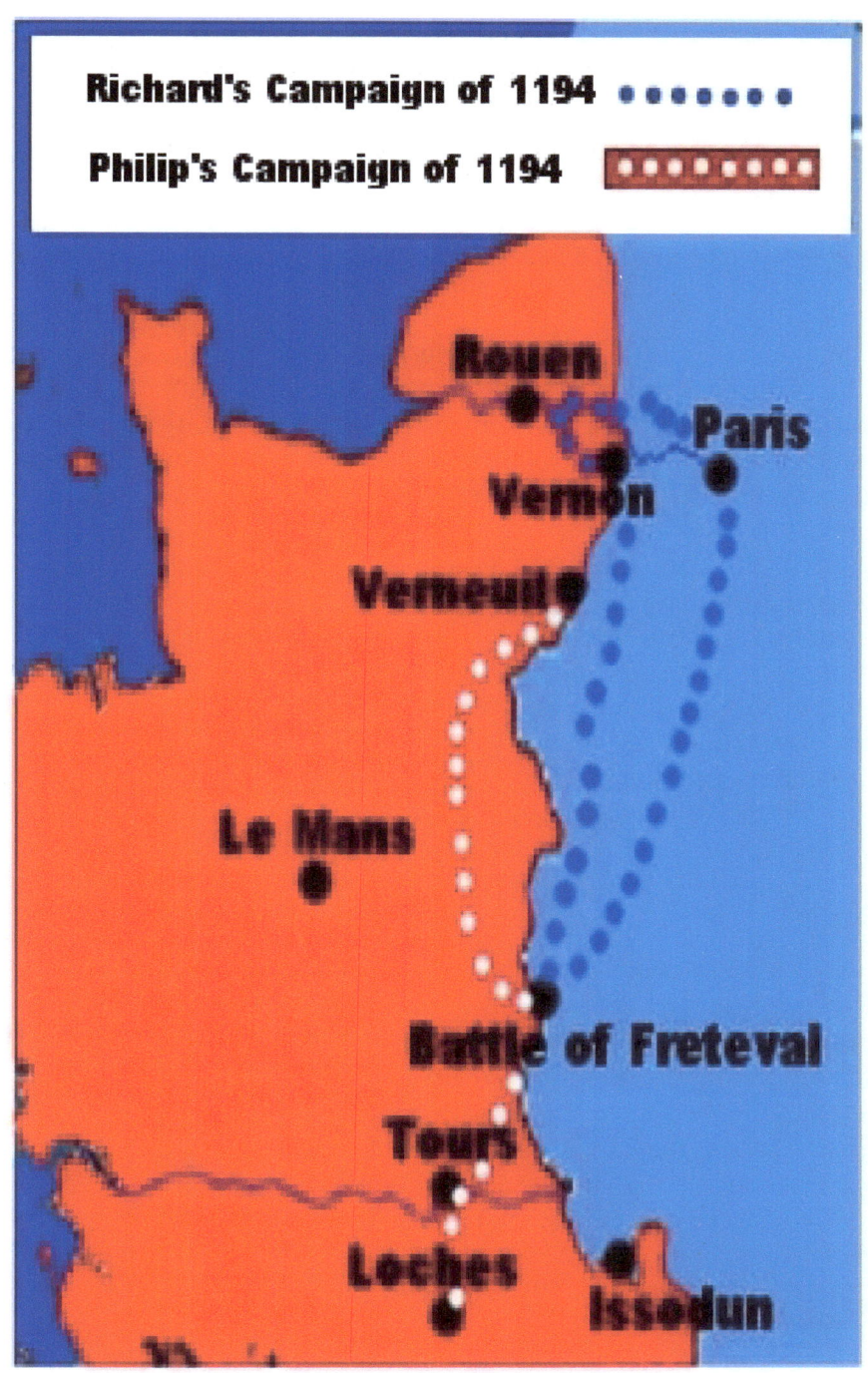

Campaign map in Western France of 1194 A

Richard showed his usual fearless courage during the battle, but also his experience as a general by putting Sir William Marshal in command of the reserve, which hovered the battlefield incase of a French counter attack. Richard acclaimed after the battle;

> "The Marshal did better than all of you, if there had been trouble he would have been there, when one has a reserve one does not fear the enemy".

Philip sieving from his defeat at Fretéval, regrouped the remainder of his forces in Ile de France and launched a vengeful attack on Normandy. Richard had left Prince John and the Earl of Arundel in charge of the defence of the Duchy. When they heard that King Philip and the French forces were advancing towards Rouen they gathered together the troops in the vicinity and intercepted them just south of the capital at Vaudreuil. The two mounted retinues smashed into each other, using sword, lance and axe to try and gain the advantage, but in the ensuing skirmish the French knights managed to force to Anglo-Norman forces from the field. They however sustained heavy losses and King Philip decided to call off the advance towards Rouen. With the campaigning season coming to an end a truce was agreed at Tillieres in which both sides agreed to keep what they held at the present time.

1195 AD, Total War

In 1195 AD Richard was in Rouen preparing for the second phase of the war. Rumours were rife that the German Emperor Henry IV who had just completed the conquest of Southern Italy and Sicily intended to add the Kingdom of France to his Empire. He indeed sent the Lionheart a present of a golden crown requesting that Richard attack the lands of the French King. Richard sent his diplomatic envoy the Bishop of Ely to the German court in order to enquire what Henry was up too. King Philip realising the danger of fighting a war on two fronts tried to apprehend the Bishop and declared the current truce null and void. He took the offensive and attacked Eastern Normandy from Gisors and the French controlled castles of the Vexin.

King Richard I, Normandy 1194 AD

1195 AD, Vaudreuil

Mediators on both sides had been working hard to try and implement a permanent truce which culminated in the peace talks between the two sovereigns at Vaudreuil. The French engineers who had been besieging the castle continued their work in secret of undermining the castle walls during the ongoing negotiations
An almighty crash was heard as the castle's stone defences came crashing down in a cloud of dust and rumble. Richard stormed out and swore by God's legs he would have revenge. He immediately gathered his men and charged the French lines, overrunning their positions, capturing many of Philip's Knights. As Philip retreated, the bridge over the Seine collapsed from under him. Philip not for the last time only just escaped from being drowned.

Richard retaliated and took the war to Philips lands across the border in France. He ravaged the French controlled Vexin, villages were sacked, crops burned, vines pulled up and all who resisted put to the sword. The fighting only ended when disturbing news from Spain reached the two Kings. Boyac the Muslim Emir in North Africa had invaded Spain and defeated the King of Castile. The Pope urged both Kings to put aside their differences and help Castile against the Moors in Iberia.
At Louviers Richard and Philip met to consummate a more long lasting peace. Richard handed back Philip's Sister Alice and a marriage was planned between Richard's niece and Philip's son Louis. The agreement was delayed until the German Emperor ratified the terms, as Richard was still Henry's man because of his oath of fealty when he was a prisoner in Germany. Henry sent back the Bishop of Ely with instructions that there should be no peace between England and France. He also gave Richard 17000 marks to continue the war along with the title "Vicar of Arles". In theory this would have made Richard ruler of most of Southern France including the important port of Marseilles. Although the territory was part of the German Empire, in practice Henry did not have the power to impose it. While Richard was in Chinon, Anjou Philip sent assassins (15 in total) to kill him. The plot failed, but the personal enmity between the two Kings was highly clear.

In November King Philip attacked the Norman port of Dieppe, the town was burned to the ground and using "Greek fire" and several English Ships were destroyed in the harbour. Although it was high winter both sides continued to raid and counter raid.

The French raid on Dieppe 1195

In the Berry region of central France Richard's mercenary captain Marcadier captured the important town and castle of Issoudun. Philip sent south a relief force. His men recaptured the town, but were unable to budge the stubborn Angevin garrison, who took refuge behind the castle walls. As the French surrounded the castle and began preparations for a long drawn out siege, King Richard organised a relief force led by him personally. He marched off from Normandy and within three days he arrived and broke through the siege lines, relieving the castle and his mercenary captain Marcadier.

1196 AD, My beautiful Daughter Château Gaillard
(La roche d'Andeli)

1196 AD into the third year of war Richard had regained most of the territory lost to Philip with the exception of the Vexin. The problem remained that Philip was still in control of Gisors and within striking distance of Rouen. Richard's solution to this problem would antagonise the uneasy peace.

Philip had demanded the fief of Andely which was under the jurisdiction of the Archbishop of Rouen, who refused to hand it over. Richard knew if Andely fell into French hands, then Philip would control all the territory from Gisors to the Seine River. Sensing the danger, Richard took the initiative and seized the town. He immediately commenced the construction of Chateau Gaillard (Le Roche d'Andeli)

View towards the inner bailey of Château Gaillard

Richard could now turn the tables against Philip with the construction of Chateau Gaillard. The town of Andely is located where the rivers Gambon and Seine converge in the middle of the Vexin. Richard built his new castle to be able to control river traffic into and out of Normandy and also to be within striking distance to launch attacks against Gisors and the French controlled Vexin. Perched on the cliffs above the town the castle was a masterpiece of military engineering and one of the most modern castles built in the twelfth century. Although reduced to a majestic ruin today, its position and presence still dominate to Seine valley and the surrounding area.

Donjon en bec, the keep of Château Gaillard

All of Richards experience and knowledge of warfare went into the construction. The keep (Donjon en bec) presented a solid pointed edge towards the inner bailey and a concave rear on the cliff side above the river Seine. The inner bailey was cut straight out of the rock base and topped with an impressive corrugated stone wall.

During the building a shower of blood from the heavens spattered the walls. Richard ordered the continuation of the work and said:

"God himself would not stop the construction of the castle".

In an amazing 13 months the construction of the castle and fortified town was complete. Richard remarked;

"How beautiful my one year old daughter has grown".

Château Gaillard, Eure, Normandy

Chateau Gaillard cost over (£11.000 pounds) an enormous amount of money at the time, dwarfing all the other construction projects in the Angevin Empire. Expensive as it was, it was worth it and would remain Richard's favorite headquarters until his death. Legend has it that Philip came the see the castle and shouted to Richard;

"Even if the walls were made of iron I could take the castle"

Richard replied back;

"Even if the walls were made of butter I could hold it".

Sadly Philip never dared attack the castle while Richard was alive. The continuation of the conflict in 1196 AD saw Richard's young nephew Arthur of Brittany being smuggled into Philip's hands.

Reconstruction of how the castle may have looked. Photo taken from the Chateau Gaillard tourist panel,

Richard at once invaded Brittany with a large host and forced the Bretons to submit and change sides, forming an alliance with him against the French King

The Lionheart also captured and destroyed the town of Vierzon (Berry) whose lord had recently appealed directly to King Philip over a dispute. Richard was sending out a message to all of his vassals that they could not count on the Judaification or protection by the King of France anymore in grievances against him. Richard named his nephew Otto of Brunswick (who was actually born in Normandy) as Count of Poitou to strengthen international family ties.

There was also a welcome breakthrough in the south. After much negotiating the marriage between Richard's sister Joan (once of Sicily) and the new Count of Toulouse ended the feud between the Angevins (Dukes of Aquitaine) and the Counts of Toulouse. Philip had lost his only great ally against Richard in the south of France. Enraged by the news, he again descended on the Duchy of Normandy, this time from the north attacking the border town of Aumale, and then occupying Nonancourt on the border.

The tit for tat continued to rage back and forth, Prince John subdued Philip's success by capturing the castle of Gamaches in the Vexin.

Richard decided to advance along the Seine valley upstream from Chateau Gaillard and successfully attacked the important town of Gaillon.

Although he was very careful not to put is men in any danger the same cannot be said about his own personal safety. In the assault on the walls, leading from the front he was wounded by a crossbow bolt to the knee.

Gaillon castle captured by King Richard I in 1196 AD

1197 AD
The wheel of fortune turns against Philip

1197 AD was a defining year in the war between King Richard and King Philip. Since 1194 AD Richard had slowly been turning the tide against Philip, gaining back the lost ground and forging alliances both internally and externally. The seeds of these alliances came to fruition in late 1196 and 1197 AD.

When Richard was a prisoner in Germany he had forged a personal friendship with the Rhineland Princes, this relationship would in time put pressure on France's northern front, especially the Count of Flanders. By 1197 AD the economic blockade of Flanders forced Count, Baldwin to ditch his allegiance to King Philip in order to avoid economic disaster.

Richard also gave Baldwin 5,000 marks of silver to pursue the war against his former master King Philip.

Spring came with the renewal of hostilities. This time Richard took to war to Philip by raiding the town of Saint Valery on France's northern coast. The town was burned to the ground and the relics of Saint Valery were taken away to Normandy. During the raid some English ships were found breaking the embargo, bringing supplies to Richard's enemies. The English sailors were hung, their cargos seized and distributed amongst Richard's supporters and their ships sunk.

Richard King of England (14th century manuscript)

Beauvais and Milly

Richard's brother Prince John had been given the task of harrying the lands around Beauvais on Normandy's North Eastern frontier.

The warlike Bishop of Beauvais had long been an enemy of Richard and had been part of Philip's diplomatic mission when the Lionheart was held captive in Germany. Prince John, Mercadier and Sir William Marshal ravaged the Bishop's lands. Just outside the gates of Beauvais they put to flight the local militia and captured the erstwhile Bishop in the process.

They then proceeded to assault the nearby castle of Milly sur Therain. This was where Sir William Marshal (now over fifty years of age) became the hero of the day, once again. Upon seeing a brave young Flemish knight fighting alone on the battlements of Milly in mortal danger, Marshal leapt forward into the fray. He scaled the castle walls and single handedly drove off the knight's attackers. When the castle's castellan tried to counter attack, Marshal beat him to the ground and then sat on him while waiting for reinforcements to arrive.

Marshal's actions helped galvanise the Anglo-Normans to redouble their efforts and force open the castle gates, taking the fortress by storm. The jubilant Anglo-Norman routiers destroyed the castle, taking their booty and prisoners back with them over the border into Normandy.

Beauvais cathedral, France

Sir William Marshal defending a Flemish Knight on the castle battlemounts of Milly sur Therain

Flanders, Northern France

Marshal was sent north to seal the diplomatic ties with Count Baldwin and the other major noble families of Flanders. The Flemish army invaded the county of Artois, captured the town of Douai and commenced the siege of the region's capital Arras. King Philip now faced with a total collapse of royal authority, gathered together his army and marched north to deal with the Flemish.

Arms of Flandres

He raised the siege and pursued Count Baldwin back into Flanders. By Ypres, Baldwin set a trap for Philip luring him further into Flanders, stretching his supply lines. He gave orders for the bridges in front and behind of King Philip's army to be destroyed trapping the French.

Philip tried to worm his way out of the situation by acclaiming he had come to make peace with the Count; his pleas fell on dear ears, Baldwin forced him to surrender.

He was lucky Richard was campaigning in Auvergne

Count Baldwin of Flanders, 14th century manuscript

(taking 10 castles off the King of France) or he may well have been taken prisoner and ransomed off to the English King.

In September Count Baldwin and the leading magnates of Flanders came to Chateau Gaillard to consummate their alliance with King Richard. Philip who was supposed to attend refused; reneging on all the promises he had made with Count Baldwin and returned to Paris. During the same month Henry VI, the German Emperor died, leaving his infant son as heir to the imperial throne. An ensuing power struggle followed between Henry's brother Phillip Duke of Swabia, who received support from the King of France and Otto de Brunswick (Richard's nephew) who received Angevin Support.

Otto IV, stained glass window, Strasbourg

1198 AD, The Lion and the Lamb

The election of the new Emperor side tracked events in Normandy in the beginning of 1198 AD. During the same year Innocent III became the new Pope in Rome. On his agenda was firstly to re-establish the power of the Papacy and secondly to destroy the power of the German Emperor in Italy and Sicily, who were becoming far too powerful too tolerate anymore from the Papacy's point of view.

Richard's candidate and nephew Otto de Brunswick (Son of Henry "the Lion" and Matilda Plantagenet) offered concessions in order to gain the support of the Holy Father in Rome against the Hohenstaufen candidate. The Lionheart also used his influence with the intention of going on Crusade again which deeply pleased the Pope.

Innocent had also taken up the cause of King Philip's estranged wife princess Ingeborg of Denmark,

Arms of Otto IV, Historia Anglorum

whom the French King had repudiated since their marriage in 1193 AD. King Philip tried to marry Agnes of Merania a German princess to counter Richard's recent political successes, but it was to no avail as the Pope declared the marriage illegal as Philip was still married to Ingeborg.

By July Otto had been crowned in Cologne by the Bishop as the new Holy Roman Emperor and King Philip was on the verge of being excommunicated because of the unjust treatment of his wife. With only one cause of action left open to him, he embarked on a military campaign to restore authority and confidence in his rule.

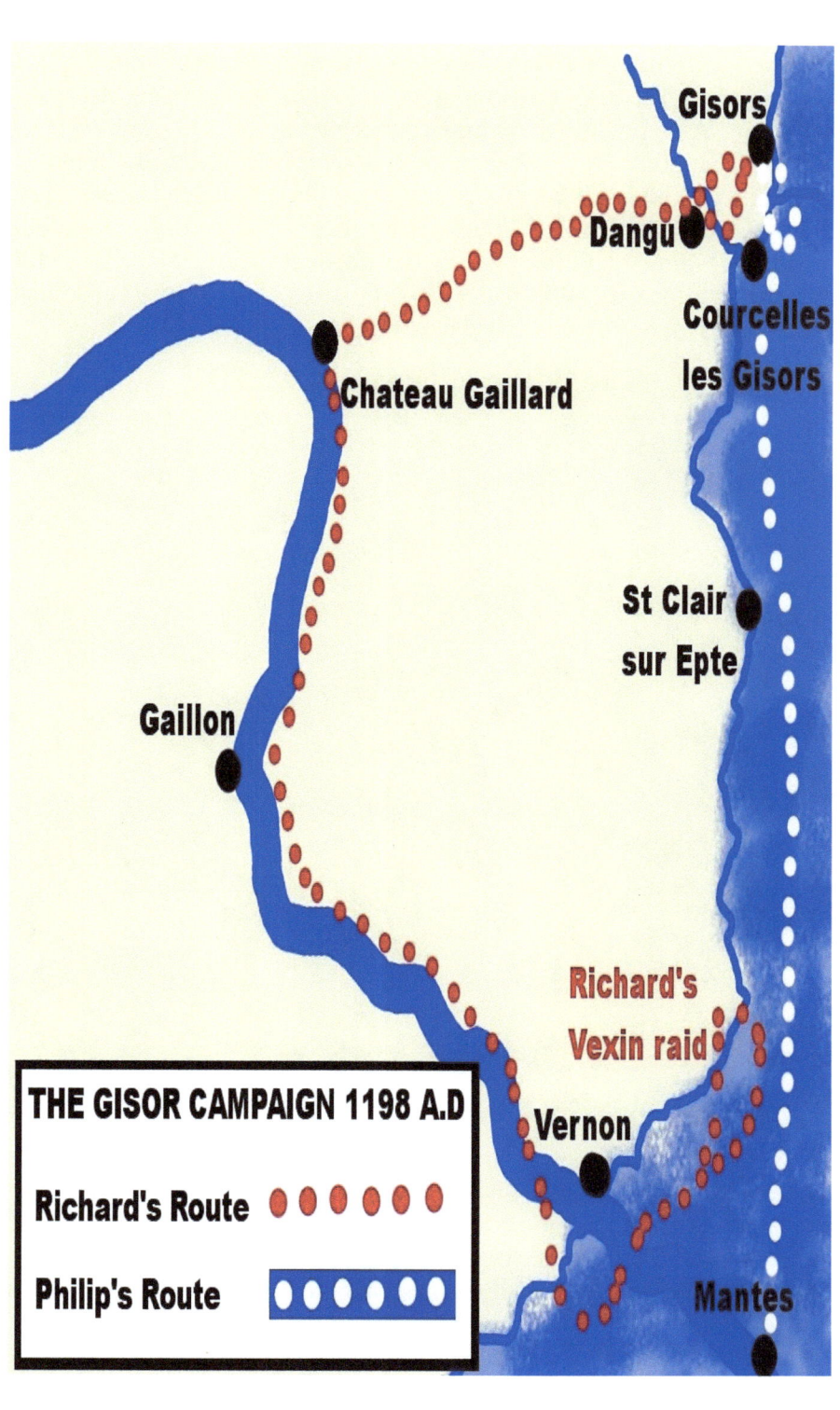

Flanders was out of the question because of its proximity to the German Empire and Philip dared not risk antagonisng its new Emperor. Also Count Baldwin had followed up his victories of 1197 AD by reducing the last remaining Royal French strongholds in Flanders. This time there was no relief force to save Arras. The Flemings took the capital of Artois by force along with many other towns including St Omer. With the north basically closed off for any operations King Philip decided the best strategy was to attack Eastern Normandy from the French Vexin.

The Battle of Gisors 1198 AD

The motte of the castle of Gisors, Eure, Normandy

In the summer of 1198 AD King Philip suffered another defeat at the hands of the English King. Somewhere in the Seine valley between Jumieges and Vernon a skirmish took place in which Philip lost over sixty knights and forty plus men at arms. The French army including the King were forced to flee, and were chased all the way back to the border fortress of Vernon.

Following up this victory Richard invaded the French Vexin, destroyed the harvest and captured the castle of Courcelles les Gisors. The castle was an important part of a chain of fortresses that followed the river Epte and then river Eure towards the Seine at La Roche Guyon. While it remained in Angevin hands, its garrison could hamper and disrupt supply and communications between the other French controlled castles.

The overgrown ruins of Courcelles les Gisors castle

The Lionheart sent them back to Dangu to mobilise the main army, while he and a small contingent of knights went forth to observe King Philip's movements. On accessing the situation, and against the advice of some of his men to wait for the reinforcements to arrive, Richard leapt forward on his war horse and charged directly at the French.

"Like a hungry Lion upon its prey"

Like a hungry lion upon its prey Richard charged into the fray, cutting through deep into the ranks of the surprised French army.

So fierce was the charge that the French soldiers buckled under the pressure and began to panic. Richard and his knights hacked their way towards the Fleur des Lys banner and King Philip himself. Philip fearing for his life panicked and trampled down his own men in order to escape the carnage. He could not believe what was happening and rode directly to reach the safety of Gisors castle. Richard relentlessly pursued him and unhorsed three of his knights (Matthew de Morenci, Fulk de Gilerval and Alan de Rusci) with a single lance. Before the town gates could be opened the bridge on which the French knights were gathering collapsed from under their weight. King Philip fell into the river head first and had to be dragged out to avoid being drowned. The remnants of his army lay shattered; some dead in the rout, some drowned in the river and others were captured. Over thirty knights were led off into captivity and may well have been executed by Mercadier who believed no ransom would be forth coming.

Later arms of King Richard I

It seemed even God had forsaken King Philip as Richard said:

"It was not I who had defeated the French, but God as we are fighting a just cause".

This is where England's national motto stems from **"Dieu et Mon Droit" (God and my right).** King Richard no longer considered himself a vassal of the King of France, but unto God himself. With a lack of siege equipment Richard returned triumphantly back to Chateau Gaillard with the victorious campaign of 1198 AD at an end.

The Battle of Gisors 1198 AD from the "Chroniques de France ou de Saint Denis"

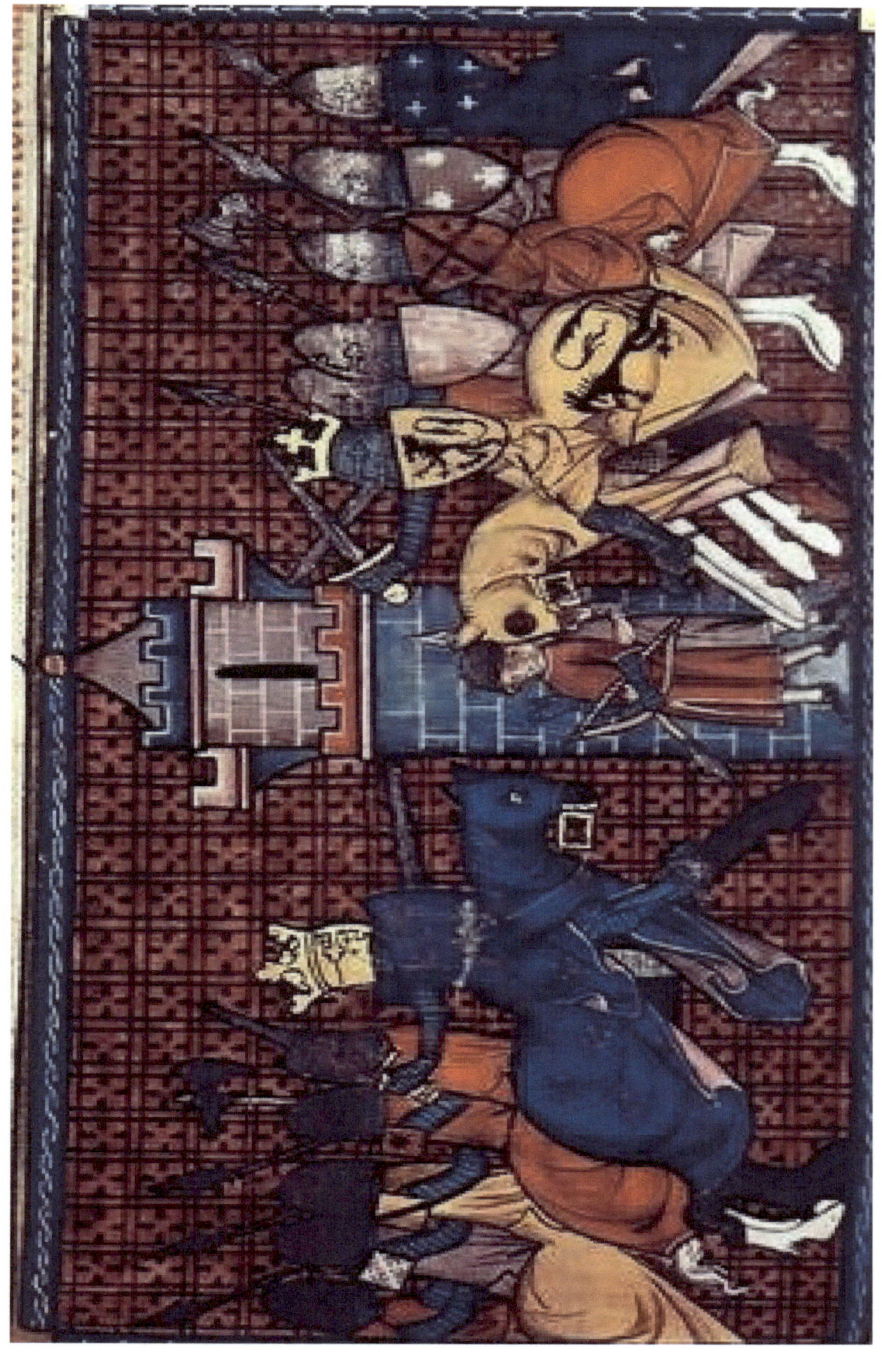

1199 AD, The uneasy peace and the end of the Lionheart

In the winter of 1198 AD Walter Hubert, Archbishop of Canterbury came to Normandy apparently by the request of King Philip to arrange a permanent peace between the two Kings. In January Richard who was at Domfont on Normandy's southern Frontier marched off to Chateau Gaillard to seal the peace with King Philip. The hatred between the two Kings was so strong that the Treaty had to be concluded with Richard coming to the river Seine from Andeli by boat and Philip on horseback on the other side of the river.

In the end only a truce for five years could be agreed. The truce was nearly broken when Marcadier and his routiers were attacked while crossing the lands of the King of France; Philip denied all connections concerning this cowardly attack. In early spring 1199 AD Philip started the construction of a new castle by Gaillon, taking wood from the forest which belonged to the Normans. King Richard collected his army and forced Philip to dismantle the castle before war was declared. With the situation stabilised in Normandy the Lionheart headed south into Anjou, then Poitou while emissaries from England and France tried to hammer out a permanent peace.

The Legend of the lost Gold

Legend has it that a peasant in Limousin found a horde of Roman gold. The treasure found its way into the hands of the local Lord Achard of Chalus a vassal of the Count of Limoges, who was in turn a vassal of King Richard. Some of this treasure should have been handed over to Richard, but Achard refused. Richard laid siege to the castle of Chalus Charbol. The garrison offered to surrender the castle if they were to be allowed to go free. Richard was so angered by their boldness that he swore to take the castle by force and execute the entire garrison. Richard and Marcadier reconnoitered the castle looking for the weakest point. During this scouting mission a cook picked up a crossbow and took aim, hitting the King in his shoulder.

King Richard had been careless in not wearing his armour, broke off the arrow and taunted the garrison. It seemed this was just another minor incident as the King and Marcadier rode back to camp.

The King's doctor (who became known as the butcher) tried to remove the arrow head, but infected the wound in doing so. Gangrene or septicemia set in and the Lionheart was on borrowed time. He sent word for Eleanor his mother to come to him, knowing the situation was serious. When the castle fell to Richard's forces he asked for the man who had shot him to be brought forward.

Richard asked:

> **"What harm have I done to you 'so that you have tried to kill me"**

The cook replied/

> **"You have killed my father and my brothers and you would have killed me"**

Magnanimous to the end the Lionheart forgave him and ordered the man to be set free. On the 6th of April King Richard made his last rites to his chaplain Milo.

He had not confessed in seven years because he could not let go the hatred he fostered for King Philip of France. He asked to be forgiven for the wrongs he had done against his father and died. The unfortunate cook who had been set free by Richard was arrested by Marcadier and flayed alive. Eleanor mourned her favorite son and acclaimed:

"I have lost the staff of my age and the light of my life"

King Richard was laid to rest in the Abbey of Fontevraud, beside his father. His brain was buried at Charroux Abbey in Poitou, his body lay in rest at Fontevraud abbey in Anjou and the heart of the great warrior was given to the Cathedral of Rouen in Normandy, For England there was nothing just the legend.

Lead box containing the remains of Richard's heart found in Rouen Cathedral, photo credit: Musée départemental des Antiquités © Yohann Deslandes/CG76

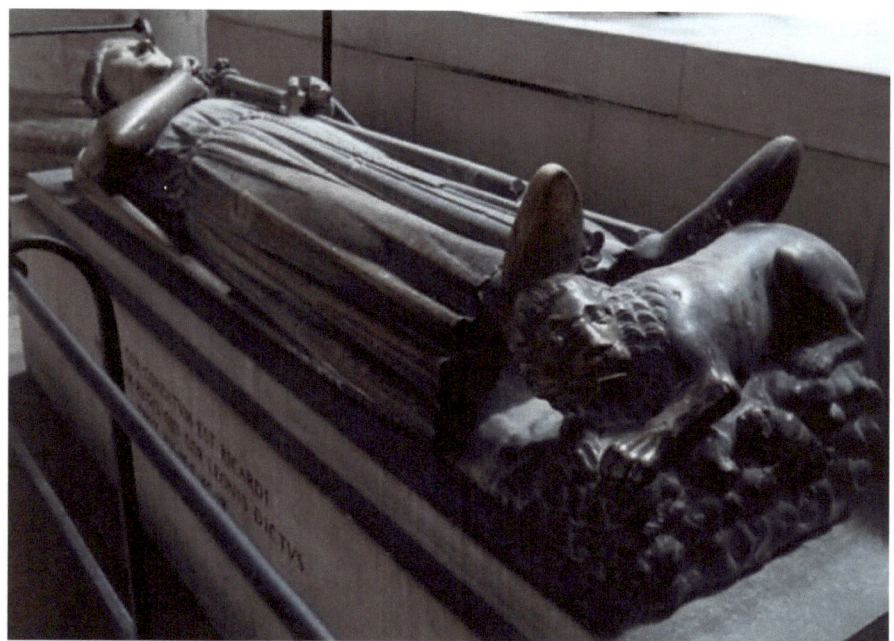

Effigy of Richard I in Rouen Cathedral, Normandy

Aftermath

Had Richard survived, the war would have recommenced at some stage. If the last six years were anything to go by King Richard would probably have extinguished the Kingdom of France, but that will remain one of histories what ifs?

Prince John was in Brittany when he heard the news of Richard's death. He rode directly to Chinon to seize the Royal treasury and then went on to the Abbey of Fontevrault to pay his respects to his brother. On his way north he found that King Philip had already started to stir up trouble in Le Mans, declaring for Arthur of Brittany's' (John's nephew) claim to the throne. John managed to get to Normandy where by chance the two most respected men in the Angevin Empire (Sir William Marshal and Hubert Walter, the Archbishop of Canterbury) were waiting for him. Although the Archbishop preferred Arthur's claim, Marshal stated that he was still a boy and emphatically advocated John's cause. In the end Marshal got his way and cleared the way for John to become King.

On the 22nd of May 1200 AD at Le Goulet on the River Seine King Philip accepted John as the rightful heir to all of Richard's fiefs held in France.

For the time being Philip was content not to disturb the peace of Le Goulet, his war with Richard had bleed him dry and he needed time to rebuild his resources before contemplating an attack on the Angevin Empire. By 1202 AD however the situation had changed and Philip used a dispute between King John and one of his vassals (the Lusignans) to exercise his right as John's Overlord in France.

Effigy of King John, Richard's heir and successor

In the war that followed John was driven from his ancestral lands in France. In the summer of 1203 AD Philip laid siege to Chateau Gaillard. An attempted plan to relieve the castle failed and slowly the garrison under the command of Sir Roger de Lacy began to fear the worst. In March 1204 AD the impregnable Chateau Gaillard fell, its capture signaled the end of Anglo-Norman rule in Normandy which had lasted for nearly 200 years. Only the Channel Islands held out and remained crown lands. John had undone all of his brother's good work. The simple fact was that although John was a capable ruler he was not in Richards's league.

A comment from the chronicles of William Marshal states:

"The Normans in the days of old were grain, but now they are like chaff since the death of King Richard, they have had no leadership. With the Lionheart gone, the Normans were blown about by a puff of wind from France"

Other titles in the series

"The Normans"

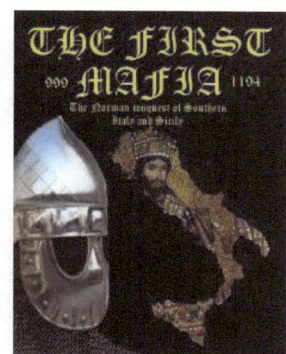

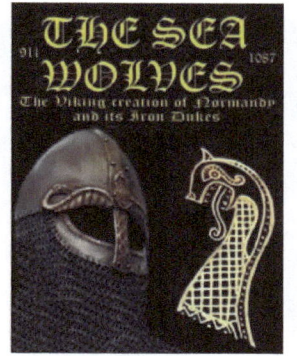

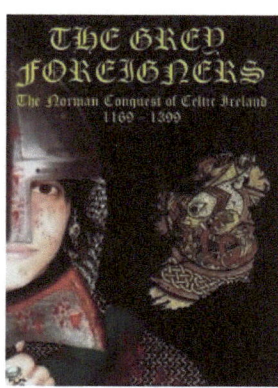
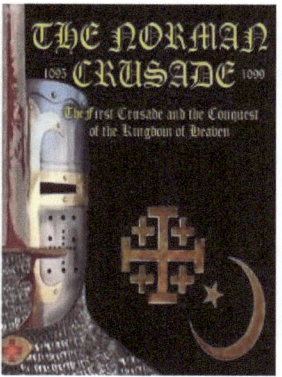
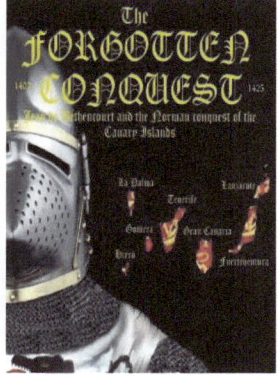

Other titles from the author

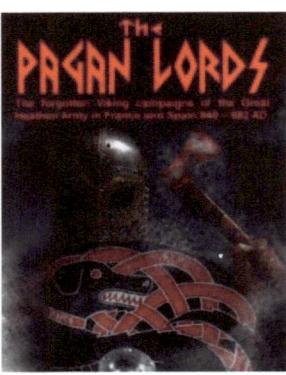
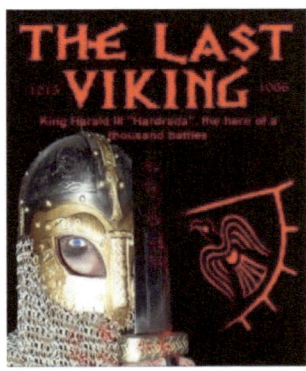

THE LAST PRINCE
Wales' Braveheart, Owain Glyndwr, the last Welsh Prince of Wales

THE GREAT HEATHEN ARMY
Ivar "the Boneless" and the Viking invasion of Britain"

THE PAGAN LORDS
"The forgotten Viking campaigns of the Great Heathen Army in France and Spain"

THE LAST VIKING
King Harald III "Hardrada" the hero of a Thousand battles